IMAGES
of America

ANSLEY PARK

In this c. 1946 photograph, comedian Bob Hope playfully takes his frustration out on his putter during an exhibition golf game at the Ansley Golf Club. In his book *Confessions of a Hooker: My Lifelong Love Affair with Golf*, Hope stated, "I get upset over a bad shot just like everyone else. But it's silly to let the game get to you. When I miss a shot, I just think what a beautiful day it is . . . then I take a breath. I have to do that. That's what gives me strength to break the club." (Courtesy of Bob Hope Enterprises.)

ON THE COVER: The brick house at 58 Fifteenth Street (now 178 Fifteenth Street) cost about $10,000 when it was constructed sometime after May 31, 1907. In 1908–1909, it was the residence of William O. and Fannie E. Jones. William owned a livery stable located at 35 South Forsyth Street. In this postcard image from the early 1900s, a carriage with a liveried driver is parked at the curb. (Author's collection.)

IMAGES
of America

ANSLEY PARK

Donald L. Ariail

ARCADIA
PUBLISHING

Published by Arcadia Publishing
Charleston, South Carolina

Library of Congress Control Number: 2012956006

For all general information, please contact Arcadia Publishing:
Telephone 843-853-2070
Fax 843-853-0044
E-mail sales@arcadiapublishing.com
For customer service and orders:
Toll-Free 1-888-313-2665

Visit us on the Internet at www.arcadiapublishing.com

This book is dedicated to my wife, Karen;
our children, Greg, Don, and Melissa;
and our grandchildren, Asher, Kennedy, Jackson, Taylor, and Dylan.

CONTENTS

ACKNOWLEDGMENTS

This book was made possible by former residents of the neighborhood and organizations that provided me with historical information, images, and editorial input and graciously gave of their time. I am forever grateful to the following contributors (not listed in order of importance): David Sheppard, Paula Savignano, Bill Ellis, Art Benton, and David Swann at Ansley Golf Club; David Gambrell; Bill Lyons at First Presbyterian Church; Tallulah Reed Lyons; Ann Tuffs-Church at First Church of Christ, Scientist; Greg Germani at the Atlanta Time Machine; Carrie Edwards and Patty Gregory at Children's Healthcare of Atlanta at Scottish Rite; E. Fay Pearce Jr.; Brittany Harper at the Center for Puppetry Arts; Sarah Berman at The Breman Jewish Heritage Museum; Mark Jacobson and Janice Blumberg at The Temple; Reverend Bob Tyler at Peachtree Christian Church; Crystal Butts at the Georgia Trust for Historic Preservation; Elizabeth Chase at Emory University; Stephen Zeitz, Peter Roberts, and Ellen Johnson at Georgia State University; Steve Engerrand and Gail Deloach at the Georgia Archives; Professor Hugh Hughes; Professor Joyce McGriff; Robert L. Foreman III; Paul Carter and Staci Catron at the Atlanta History Center; and Mary Linneman at the University of Georgia.

I would like to extend my special appreciation and thanks to Paige Adair, manager of reprographic services at the Kenan Research Center, who quickly and professionally scanned the many images acquired from the Atlanta History Center; to my son, Gregory Scott Ariail, whose editing and suggestions were incredibly helpful; and to Fay Pearce, a longtime former resident of the neighborhood, who gave the text a final review.

Last but certainly not least, I would like to thank my editor, Maggie Bullwinkel, for assisting and encouraging me at every stage of production. She kept this work moving forward!

Unless otherwise noted, all images appear courtesy of the Kenan Research Center at the Atlanta History Center.

INTRODUCTION

Ansley Park is a beautiful, historic, and unique suburb in Atlanta, Georgia. Except for brief periods of decline, it has since its birth been a prestigious place to live. It has been the residence of many of Atlanta's most distinguished men and women. Ansley Park continues to attract residents who desire to live close to the action of downtown Atlanta but prefer a quiet environment with stately homes, winding tree-lined streets, and parks. The suburb's continuing popularity was evidenced in 2011 when the American Planning Association named this midtown subdivision one of the "10 Great Neighborhoods" in America. Developed between 1904 and 1930, it was the second suburb in Atlanta (Inman Park was the first) and one of the first in the South to be built using street patterns designed to preserve the natural contours of the land and to incorporate a mixture of housing types—mansions, one- and two-story houses, bungalows, apartments, and now condominiums.

Webster's dictionary defines "neighborhood" as: "the vicinity; a district of a particular kind; the persons in a locality." Accordingly, this book includes brief pictorial histories of the 275-acre neighborhood, as well as nearby institutions and areas, and selected residents. The story of Ansley Park begins 40 years after the 1864 destruction of Atlanta during the Civil War. This conflict took place quite literally on the doorstep of the future suburb. A decade before Ansley Park's construction began, Piedmont Park, which borders the suburb, was the site of the 1895 Cotton States and International Exposition. The war and the exposition, which set the stage for the suburb's development, are portrayed in the first two chapters. The next two chapters include a history of the suburb's birth and of selected houses and residents.

Chapter five is devoted to a snapshot history of Margaret Mitchell, the Pulitzer Prize–winning author of *Gone With the Wind*, who lived most of her life in and around Ansley Park. She was living in the suburb at the time of her tragic death in 1949. With many of the suburb's residents having been members of social organizations in the area, chapter six provides short histories of the Piedmont Driving Club, founded in 1887, the Ansley Golf Club, founded in 1912, and the Atlanta and Habersham Chapters of the Daughters of the American Revolution, founded, respectively, in 1891 and 1922.

Chapter seven includes short histories of First Church of Christ, Scientist, erected in the suburb in 1914, and three of the four still-standing nearby houses of worship: First Presbyterian Church, completed in 1919; Peachtree Christian Church, dedicated in 1928; and The Temple, dedicated in 1931. A prominent feature in the suburb is Woodberry Hall, which was originally constructed in 1914 as a school for girls but was converted to apartments in 1940. Chapter eight tells the story of this school and one of its prominent long-term residents, Dorothy Alexander, who founded the Atlanta Ballet. This chapter also includes the history of Spring Street School, constructed in 1919 to service the educational needs of the growing suburb. Lastly, chapter nine touches upon the 12 Georgia governors who lived in the Governor's Mansion on The Prado, the previous residence of Edwin P. Ansley, the suburb's developer.

Having grown up on the periphery of Ansley Park, the author has many fond memories of this beautiful neighborhood and the surrounding area. It is the author's intention for this work to complement the written and pictorial histories previously published about this Atlanta neighborhood.

One

CIVIL WAR

In 1860, forty-four years before the development of Ansley Park, Atlanta was a thriving city of almost 12,000 inhabitants. Established at the southern end of the Western & Atlantic Railroad line, the town was known as Terminus from 1837 to 1843. In December 1843, it was incorporated as Marthasville, named after Martha Lumpkin Compton, the daughter of former Georgia governor Wilson Lumpkin. This painting of Atlanta by Wilbur G. Kurtz depicts the city in 1864, when, according to historian Franklin M. Garrett writing in *Yesterday's Atlanta*, "the city was one of the chief rail and industrial centers of the Confederacy." The First Union Depot, called the "Car Shed," is the long building at left center; the building with a cupola in the upper left is the combined Fulton County Courthouse and Atlanta City Hall; on the far right is the Broad Street Bridge, which was the only bridge that spanned the railroad tracks.

Confederate Generals Joseph E. Johnston (left) and John Bell Hood (below) defended Atlanta against the forces of Union General William Tecumseh Sherman. Despite the Confederate army being about half the size of the Union's, Johnston's defensive tactics proved successful in several battles. Johnston's troops, having forced Sherman into making frontal attacks, then retreated before being outflanked. When Johnston withdrew to the defenses of Atlanta, Confederate President Jefferson Davis replaced him with the aggressive John Bell Hood. Going on the offensive, Hood was unable to halt Sherman's onslaught. He then unsuccessfully tried to draw Sherman away from Atlanta by abandoning the city and cutting off the Union supply lines. Sherman occupied Atlanta on September 2, 1864. On November 15, he began his March to the Sea, a devastating tactic of "total war." (Left, courtesy of the Georgia Archives, Small Print Collection, spc03-011; below, courtesy of the Kennesaw National Battlefield Park.)

According to the *New Georgia Encyclopedia*, "Confederate preparations for a system of defense against the Union forces included a fortified perimeter around Atlanta, which was ten miles in circumference and positioned about a mile outside of the city." The 1863–1864 photographs on this page depict two of these fortifications. A Georgia historical marker located a short distance from the present Rhodes Hall entrance to Ansley Park indicates that Confederate forces built trench works on the south boundary of Collier Woods. From this position on July 20, 1864, "the troops of Walker's and Bate's divisions of Hardees' Corps advanced north to attack Federal forces posted near Collier Road in the Battle of Peachtree Creek." This encounter was General Hood's first indecisive battle against the forces of General Sherman. (Above, courtesy of the Library of Congress.)

A postcard image of a section of the diorama at the Cyclorama (above) depicts fighting at the Hurt House during the Battle of Atlanta on July 22, 1864. In this one-day battle, the estimated casualties were 9,100—approximately 3,600 for the Union and 5,500 for the Confederates. After General Hood's four engagements with the Union Army (the Battles of Peachtree Creek, Atlanta, Ezra Church, and Jonesboro) failed to stop Sherman, the Confederates evacuated the city on September 1, 1864. The Union Army occupied Atlanta until November 15. According to Franklin Garrett, the below lithograph of Atlanta's occupation "shows what is now Five Points from Marietta Street looking northeast; Decatur Street is on the right, Peachtree Street at center, and Edgewood Avenue, then called Cherokee Street, at left center." (Above, author's collection.)

The evacuation of civilians ordered by General Sherman on September 4 was completed by September 20. The 1864 photograph at right shows a procession of covered wagons on Peachtree Street leaving Atlanta. The Georgia Railroad Bank is the building next to the tracks in the right foreground. The photograph below, taken sometime in 1864, shows a hectic evacuation scene at the Car Shed. Sherman's army severely damaged the city on November 14, the night before embarking on its March to the Sea.

The undated photograph at left shows some of the war's aftermath. According to the Georgia History Center, "40 percent of Atlanta lay in ruins." By 1865, the city had begun its recovery. Below, activity is seen on Peachtree Street after some rebuilding had taken place. However, remnants of the destruction are still evident in this photograph. The burned-out building in the right foreground is what remained of the Georgia Railroad Bank. The vacant lot to the right of the Billiard Saloon is where the Atlanta Hotel had stood. (Left, courtesy of the Georgia Archives, Vanishing Georgia Collection, ful1091-94.)

Two

PIEDMONT PARK

Following Atlanta's devastation during the Civil War, civic leaders were eager to showcase their resurrected city. In the late 19th century, expositions were a popular way to attract visitors and business. Atlanta hosted three such expositions: the 1881 International Cotton Exposition, held in Oglethorpe Park; and the 1887 Piedmont Exposition and 1895 Cotton States and International Exposition, both held at the future site of Piedmont Park. The land on which the 1887 and 1895 expositions were held was then owned by the Piedmont Driving Club. The 189 acres of the park were subsequently purchased by the city of Atlanta. Teams representing the University of Georgia and the Georgia School of Technology (Georgia Tech), and Atlanta's first professional baseball team, the Atlanta Crackers, played their first games at the baseball fields constructed in 1898. Piedmont Park is located across Piedmont Avenue from Ansley Park. This *Harpers Weekly* illustration by Frank Leslie depicts officers and buildings of the 1887 Exposition. (Courtesy of Special Collections and Archives, Georgia State University.)

Grover Cleveland, who served two terms as president of the United States (1885–1889 and 1893–1897), attended both the 1897 and 1895 expositions. This 1895 photograph shows the president (foreground) walking in front of the Georgia Building. According to the *New Georgia Encyclopedia*, "a crowd of 50,000 was on hand [at the 1887 Exposition] when [Henry] Grady introduced the popular U.S. president." (Courtesy of the Georgia Archives, Vanishing Georgia Collection, ful0674.)

The 1895 Cotton States and International Exposition opened on September 18, 1895. During its three-month existence, it attracted some 800,000 visitors. Although not as successful as hoped, "the Cotton States Exposition did showcase Atlanta as a regional business center and helped to attract investment" according to the *New Georgia Encyclopedia*. This photograph, taken from the Phoenix Wheel ride, shows many of the exposition buildings.

In 1895, Georgia played its third football game against Auburn at the Exposition Grounds in Piedmont Park. Auburn broke the tied record of one victory each by winning this game 16-6. The majority of the spectators stood on the sidelines below the main line of the Southern Railway. In the foreground, a referee wearing a cutaway coat watches the action.

This photograph of the Woman's Building shows a crowd of visitors, some of whom are disembarking from a boat docked at Clara Meer Lake. When the exposition ended, most of the buildings were demolished.

Among the 34
buildings that
comprised the
1895 Exposition
were the Art
Building (left)
and below, from
left to right, the
Electricity and
Transportation
Buildings.

The 1895 Exhibition included amusements and rides, two of which were the Phoenix Wheel (right) and Shooting the Chutes (below).

These 1895 Exposition photographs were taken in the vicinity of the Government Building and the Chime Tower. The photograph above shows three visitors standing on the walkway below the terraced area in front of the Government Building. The photograph at left, taken from a different angle, is of a crowd of visitors in front of the Government Building, which is faintly visible in the background. Note the men's bowler hats, an unidentified wheeled item (center), the fashionably dressed lady (right center), and a group of policemen (far right). (Left, courtesy of the Georgia Archives, Vanishing Georgia Collection, ful0676.)

Born into slavery in 1856, Booker T. Washington, shown here around 1903, was an influential spokesman for African Americans at the turn of the 20th century. After being freed, he worked as a janitor to help pay his way through Virginia's Hampton Normal and Agricultural Institute. In 1881, he became the first president of the Tuskegee Normal and Industrial Institute (now Tuskegee University), where he promoted industrial education for African Americans. On September 18, 1895, he delivered a speech at the opening of the 1895 Exposition. In this famous oration, he pragmatically advocated economic security and "the importance of cultivating friendly relations with the Southern white man." However, he did not advocate social equality. He stated that "in all things purely social, we can be as separate as the fingers, yet one as the hand in all things essential to mutual progress." W.E.B. DuBois, one of the founders of the NAACP, initially congratulated him on the speech. Subsequently, he and other African American leaders were highly critical of it and deridingly called it the "Atlanta Compromise." (Courtesy of the Library of Congress.)

Prior to giving the 1895 Exposition speech, which gave him national prominence, Washington was already a well-known educator and an accomplished orator. The above photograph, taken sometime between 1890 and 1915, shows him onstage speaking to a large crowd in Lakeland, state unknown. The left photograph, taken at the 1895 Exposition, is of a group of African Americans in front of the Negro's Building. In his opening-day speech, Washington spoke of the Negro Exhibition as "our humble effort at an exhibition of our progress." (Above, courtesy of the Library of Congress; left, courtesy of the Georgia Archives, Vanishing Georgia Collection, ful0668.)

Three

EARLY DEVELOPMENT

In 1875, at the age of 24, Amos Giles Rhodes moved to Atlanta. Lacking a formal education and starting with only a gold watch and $75, he became one of the South's foremost businessmen. He opened a clock and picture frame business, but soon expanded to selling furniture using the innovative installment method of financing. In 1889, he and J.J. Haverty formed the Rhodes-Haverty Furniture Company and in later years developed real estate through the Rhodes-Haverty Investment Company. While frugal in his personal habits, Rhodes was a philanthropist who gave large sums of money and land to various civic, educational, and religious organizations. This undated photograph shows Rhodes in middle age. (Courtesy of the Georgia Trust for Historic Preservation.)

Described as Romanesque Revival, the Rhodes residence (now Rhodes Hall), designed by Atlanta architect Willis F. Denny II as a composite of medieval German castles, was constructed between 1902 and 1904 at a cost of almost $50,000. Named Le Reve (the Dream), the mansion, located at 1516 Peachtree Street, was built across the street from a future entrance to Ansley Park. For many years, this was the location of the Georgia Archives, but in 1983, the building became the headquarters of the Georgia Trust for Historic Preservation. The c. 1904 drawing above shows the front of the building. The c. 1970 photograph at left shows a close-up of the exterior granite stonework. The tower, turrets, and battlements are visible in both images. (Above, courtesy of the Georgia Archives, *Rhodes Memorial Research Study* by Norman D. Askins, RG 4-11-56.)

The interior of Rhodes Hall is, according to The Georgia Trust for Historic Preservation, "one of the finest intact expressions of late Victorian design in the city." The reception area, shown above around 1904, is a focal point of this lavishly appointed mansion. The nine painted windows commemorate the rise and fall of the South during the Civil War. The three panels of the center window (right) include portraits of six Confederate leaders from Georgia and Gen. Stonewall Jackson commanding troops in 1861 at the First Battle of Manassas. The portraits are, from left to right, (top) Gen. Howell Cobb, Confederate Vice President Alexander Stephens, and Confederate Secretary of State Robert Toombs; (bottom) Gen. Clement A. Evans, Gen. John B. Gordon, and Gen. Joseph Wheeler Jr. (Above, courtesy of the Georgia Archives, *Rhodes Memorial Research Study* by Norman D. Askins, RG 4-11-56; right, courtesy of the Georgia Trust for Historic Preservation.)

This c. 1897 photograph of George Washington "Wash" Collier (center), taken at the Wash House, includes two other Atlanta pioneers, John J. Thrasher (left) and George W. Adair, a prominent name in Atlanta real estate history. Collier, who in 1845 became the second postmaster of the rapidly expanding city, had by 1863 acquired about 600 acres of land to the north of downtown Atlanta. About a third of his holding subsequently became Ansley Park.

According to *Ansley Park: 100 Years of Gracious Living*, the Wash House at 1649 Lady Marian Lane in the Sherwood Forest subdivision, adjoining Ansley Park, "is the oldest house in Atlanta still standing where it was originally built. Meredith Collier and his 10-year-old son, George Washington 'Wash' Collier, put it there along Clear Creek in 1822." These photographs show the house before and after extensive renovation.

Edwin P. Ansley was born in Augusta, Georgia, on March 30, 1866. He moved with his family to Atlanta in 1871 and then to nearby Decatur in 1874. After initially practicing law, he began a real estate career in 1890. By 1904, Ansley was a well-established real estate developer. Desiring to build a model suburb on the north side of Atlanta, Ansley in 1896 unsuccessfully tried to purchase land owned by George Washington Collier. After Collier's death in 1903, a portion of his estate came on the market. On April 6, 1904, Hugh T. Inman, a wealthy cotton broker acting on behalf of the Southern Real Estate Investment Company (SREIC), a partnership of E.P. Ansley, E.L. Douglas, W.P. Andrews, and W.F. Winecoff, purchased for $300,000 the 202.5 acres of virgin forest that comprised land lot 105. Collier had purchased this land in 1847 for $150. By the end of 1904, the SREIC had repaid Inman's loan. Ansley subsequently bought out two partners in the SREIC and became the driving force behind developing the suburb that bears his name.

In a 1903 advertising publication, *Atlanta: A Twentieth-Century City*, Edwin P. Ansley indicated that his business interests included "real estate, renting, loans and insurance." This c. 1903 photograph shows Ansley's private office in the Century Building on Alabama Street.

Brinton B. Davis, Architect.

Hotel Ansley, Atlanta, Ga.

In addition to developing Ansley Park, E.P. Ansley was involved in a number of other real estate ventures, one of which was the development of Hotel Ansley. Located at the intersection of Forsyth and Williams Streets, the hotel was constructed in 1913. This 1920s postcard image of the front and side of the hotel includes a busy street scene involving a streetcar, pedestrians, and automobiles. In 1953, the hotel was sold and the name was changed to the Dinkler Plaza Hotel. The building was demolished in 1973. (Author's collection.)

By 1905, when construction began on Ansley Park, Atlanta was again a thriving city. It had risen from the ashes of destruction and earned the motto *Resurgens* (rising again), which appears on its official seal. The population of Atlanta grew from 89,872 in 1900 to 154,839 in 1910. This growth spurred a demand for suburban housing. According to Rick Beard, "the development of Inman Park in 1889 and Ansley Park in 1904 represented the earliest manifestation of this suburban impulse in Atlanta." This c. 1904 postcard image shows pedestrians and horse-drawn vehicles on Whitehall Street. (Author's collection.)

Outside the hustle and bustle of downtown, turn-of-the-century Peachtree Street was a wide tree-lined boulevard with relatively light traffic. This c. 1905 postcard image faces north and shows Peachtree Street cutting through a quiet residential neighborhood. (Author's collection.)

After two successful auctions in 1904, the SREIC, headed by Ansley, endeavored to maintain enthusiasm by adding amenities. Rick Beard reports that "Ansley kept over two hundred men and one hundred horses and mules busy grading, clearing, and planting under the direction of Solon Z. Ruff . . . by mid-1905 [Ansley] reportedly spent . . . between $60,000 and $70,000 for improvements." Civil engineer Ruff, who had worked with the renowned landscape architect Fredric Law Olmstead on the plans for Druid Hills, a future Atlanta suburb, laid out the streets to conform to the land's natural contours. In these photographs, taken around 1905, Ruff is supervising what an advertising publication described as "batteries of transformation." He is the man holding a hat at the far left in the above photograph. Below, Ruff is visible in the center foreground.

According to Beard, land was cleared in 1905 for 15th Street, a 75-foot-wide boulevard connecting Peachtree Street to the Piedmont Driving Club, located on Piedmont Avenue. Peachtree Circle, a crescent-shaped street, would intersect Peachtree Street at two points: at Fifteenth Street on one end and close to the intersection of West Peachtree and Peachtree Street—directly in front of the home of A.G. Rhodes—at the other end. These c. 1905 photographs show men working on Peachtree Circle. In the above photograph, S.Z. Ruff is the man wearing a suit, standing alone in a small clearing between a group of mules and the tree line. Below, work is progressing near the Rhodes home, faintly visible in the center rear of the image.

In the above photograph, taken around 1905, Fifteenth Street is being graded. Below, the crowd is gathered for the third land lot auction, held on April 25, 1905. Rick Beard indicates that the auction-goers in 1905 were primarily speculators. The quick profit motive of the buyers is indicated by the rapid turnover of the lots. Of the lots sold in 1905 (39 in April and 28 in October), 24 (36 percent) were resold before they were deeded to the auction purchasers. Only four of the properties auctioned that year were occupied by the original buyers.

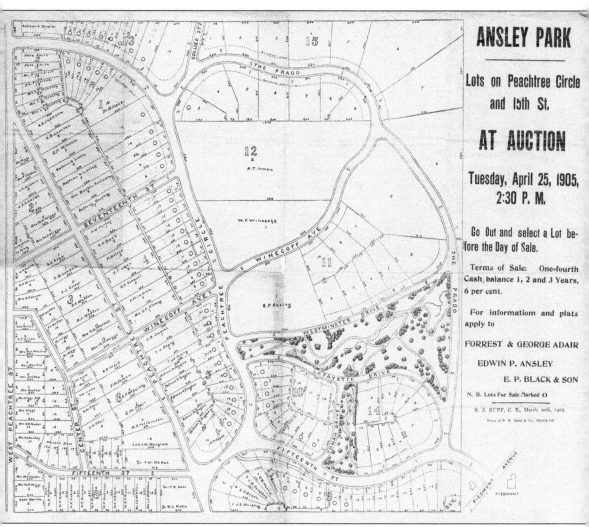

This plat by S.Z. Ruff advertised the April 25, 1905, auction of Ansley Park lots. All 51 of the lots offered for sale that day bordered the newly cut boulevards of Peachtree Circle and Fifteenth Street. This auction was the first to primarily offer lots located in what is now part of Ansley Park. The previous two auctions were mainly of lots located on Peachtree Street, West Peachtree Street, and in the triangular area between them—areas originally part of the development. (Courtesy of the Manuscript, Archives, and Rare Book Library, Emory University.)

Four

HOUSES AND RESIDENTS

Edward Hamilton Inman was heir to a fortune accumulated by his father and grandfather. His grandfather, Shadrach Inman, having lost everything during the Civil War, became a successful cotton broker. His father, Hugh Inman, prospered as a cotton broker, as the founder of a number of successful companies, and as a real estate developer. Hugh purchased the land for the Ansley Park development. Edward worked in the cotton brokerage business owned by his uncle Samuel Inman, the financier for the Inman Park development. After running unsuccessfully for mayor in 1919, Edward left the cotton business to focus on politics. His political career included service on the Fulton County Board of Commissioners and the Atlanta City Council. Pres. Woodrow Wilson appointed him to two war committees that provided advice on cotton pricing and distribution.

Designed by Edward E. Daugherty, the Tudor-styled Edward H. Inman mansion, located on Fifteenth Street, was built around 1909. The Inman family lived there until 1921, when, due to several fires at the residence, they moved to the Biltmore Hotel and began plans for the Swan House in Buckhead, to which they moved in 1928. The above photograph, taken around 1908, shows the newly constructed residence. In 1964, it was torn down to make way for the Westchester Square Development. The Sanders House, located on Lafayette Drive, is seen below around 1964. This elegant residence is composed of the renovated carriage house, stables, and outhouses of the Inman mansion. The house, which sits in a beautiful setting of woods, flowers, and a manicured lawn, borders two of Ansley's parks: Yonah Park and Winn Park.

Edwin P. Ansley was a master promoter. Throughout the development of Ansley Park, he fervently advertised the positive attributes of the development. The above advertisement, from around 1908, shows a view of Ansley Park as seen from the Inman Mansion. It promotes the subdivision's many attractions and amenities, many of which had not yet been and would not be developed. In short, Ansley proclaimed, "it has the goods." Most conspicuously, as was common for the segregated South of the era, the advertisement states that Ansley Park "has not and never will have a home belonging to a person of color or occupied by one other than a servant on the premises." The suburb remained segregated until the 1960s. The c. 1915 advertisement at right promotes the speculative atmosphere that had been prevalent since the first auction in 1904.

Elbert Tuttle (left) was a respected lawyer, a decorated brigadier general in the Army Reserve, a famous jurist, and a champion of civil rights for African Americans. He practiced law from 1923 until 1953. In 1954, he became a judge on the US Court of Appeals for the Fifth Circuit, a position he held until 1981. Tuttle was the chief judge during the turbulent period between 1960 and 1967. During that time, Judge Tuttle and his Fifth Circuit colleagues decided many of the key civil rights cases of the era. From 1981 until his death in 1996, Tuttle served on the 11th Circuit Court of Appeals. His home, seen below in 2012, was previously located on Peachtree Circle. In 1997, it escaped destruction when it was moved to 165 The Prado. (Left, courtesy of Special Collections and Archives, Georgia State University; below, author's collection.)

The above photograph shows the house at 47 Peachtree Circle around 1908. This was the home of J.T. Hall Jr. and his wife, Margarette. Hall was employed by the Carlton Shoe Company. Below, Ansley Park houses on an unpaved Peachtree Circle are seen around 1908. The third house on the right appears to be that of the Halls.

William B. Hartsfield served as mayor of Atlanta from 1937 to 1941, and again from 1942 to 1962, which is the longest tenure of any Atlanta mayor. During his six terms in office, the city's population grew tenfold. Hartsfield helped Atlanta gain a reputation as "The City Too Busy to Hate." He played a prominent role in establishing and expanding the city's airport, which in 1971 was renamed William B. Hartsfield International Airport (now Hartsfield-Jackson International Airport). Mayor Hartsfield is seen here attending a dinner party at a home on Peachtree Circle (probably the Woodberry Hall residence of the Mooars) in the 1940s or 1950s. Above, Hartsfield (right) is in the process of pinning a corsage on the lady of honor. He can be seen below, right of center in the back. (Both, courtesy of Special Collections and Archives, Georgia State University.)

J.D. Rhodes (right) was a partner
with his father, Amos, in the
furniture company A.G. Rhodes
& Son. He and his wife, Frances,
lived at what is now 228 Peachtree
Circle, a short distance from the
A.G. Rhodes mansion on Peachtree
Street. The c. 1908 photograph
below shows their two-story framed
house and, visible at the end of the
driveway, an outbuilding, possibly
a carriage house and/or servant
quarters. Chairs can be seen on
the rock porch, and a horse-drawn
carriage waits at the bottom of the
walkway steps. In 1912, this property
had an assessed value of $7,000.
(Right, courtesy of the Georgia
Trust for Historic Preservation.)

The house at One Peachtree Circle was built for Frank and Jane Ellis. This 9,000-square-foot, three-story stucco mansion, located at the intersection of Peachtree Circle and Fifteenth Street, has long been an Ansley Park icon. Designed by architect Walter Thomas Downing, the house was built in 1910 for about $20,000. The 2012 photograph above shows the house as viewed from Peachtree Circle. In the c. 1910 postcard image of Fifteenth Street below, the Ellis house is at center and the residence of W.O. Jones, at 58 Fifteenth Street (now 178 Fifteenth Street), is visible to its right. (Above, author's collection.)

Robert Troutman was a prominent Atlanta attorney and civil rights advocate. He was elected president of the Atlanta Bar Association in 1926 and of the Georgia Bar Association in 1946. According to *The Atlanta Journal*, Troutman "tried to help Georgians adapt to the 1954 U.S. Supreme Court decision ending the 'separate but equal' school systems" and sought "voluntary desegregation of Atlanta businesses and public accommodation." At right, Troutman poses for a photograph while an infantry major during World War I. The 2012 photograph below shows the Troutman residence at 132 Peachtree Circle. Listed in the National Register of Historic Places, this house was designed by the acclaimed architect Neel Reid. Another of Reid's creations, the Reid House, is visible at the top left of the photograph. (Below, author's collection.)

Dr. James Harden Crawford, an ear-eye-nose-throat specialist who attended the Atlanta Medical College, lived at 115 (now 168) Peachtree Circle with his family. Their lot abutted attorney Eugene Mitchell's mansion at 1149 Peachtree Street, the home of Margaret "Peggy" Mitchell. As a child, Dr. Crawford's daughter, Elizabeth, played with Peggy and acted in many of the fanciful plays written and produced by the future Pulitzer Prize–winning author. Bob Foreman, the grandson of Elizabeth Crawford Hitz, remembers Elizabeth saying that "Peggy always played the man." Thus, Elizabeth, called "T" by her grandchildren, considered herself Margaret Mitchell's first Scarlett. The above photograph shows the Crawford residence around 1908. The left photograph is of Elizabeth Hitz around 1968. (Left, courtesy of Robert L. Foreman III.)

Dr. Michael Hoke (right) was a pioneer orthopedist and the 1926 president of the American Orthopedic Association. According to *A Century of Better Care: 100 Years of Piedmont Hospital,* "Dr. Hoke organized Piedmont's first orthopedic department and enriched the practice of orthopedics internationally." In 1915, he was a founder and the first director of the Scottish Rite Convalescent Hospital for Crippled Children (now Children's Healthcare of Atlanta at Scottish Rite). Dr. Hoke lived at 210 Peachtree Circle and conducted his medical practice at 72 West Peachtree Street. At the request of Pres. Franklin D. Roosevelt, who suffered from polio, Dr. Hoke joined the Warm Springs Foundation as chief surgeon in 1931. Hoke's house is on the left in the c. 1908 photograph below. (Right, author's collection.)

Dr. Michael Hoke's house at 210 Peachtree Circle, seen here in 2012, was built on a lot purchased prior to the third land auction of April 25, 1905. In 1912, this property had an assessed value of $12,000. Since then, it has been expanded to approximately 7,000 square feet. For 25 years, it was owned by another Atlanta icon, Monica Kaufman Pearson, WSB-TV's highly acclaimed news anchorwoman. In July 2012, she retired after 37 years in broadcasting, including 30 years as the anchor of *Action News Nightbeat*. (Author's collection.)

Dr. E.H. Richardson Jr. and his wife, Sallie, lived in this two-story house, seen here around 1908, located at 53 East Fifteenth Street (later 179 Fifteenth Street, and since demolished). A service house and garage were added in July 1908 at a cost of $800. Rick Beard reports that in 1908, eight Ansley Park residences had servants' quarters. By 1941, there were 91 such structures. Dr. Richardson's office was at 302 Century Building.

Above, Marvin Reynolds McClatchey and his wife, Julia Anderson Nee McClatchey, pose in the 1930s. The Atlanta directories of 1916–1918 and 1923 include advertisements for Marvin's real estate business, located in the Candler Building. The undated photograph below is of the snow-covered Ansley Park home (now 224 Peachtree Circle) where the McClatcheys lived in 1938. The Atlanta directories of 1942 and 1945 list the Ansley Park residence of Juliette N. McClatchey, advertising manager of the George Muse Clothing Company and widow of Marvin McClatchey, as 157 The Prado. Other McClatchey family residents of Ansley Park included long-serving Georgia Senate secretary Devereaux Fore McClatchey II (East Park Lane) and his son Devereaux Fore McClatchey III (Avery Drive), a lawyer who served in the Georgia House of Representatives.

The brick house at 58 Fifteenth Street (now 178 Fifteenth Street), which is shown on the cover, is partially visible on the far left in the c. 1908 photograph above. This view of Fifteenth Street is from its intersection with Peachtree Circle. The early 1900s postcard image below may be a later view of this street. An early automobile is parked at the curb in front of 58 Fifteenth Street (partially visible on the left), and a horse-drawn wagon is traveling toward Piedmont Avenue. (Below, author's collection.)

Ansley Park, the finest Residence District, Atlanta, Ga.

This advertising brochure image from around 1908 shows Ansley Park as seen from the future site of Edwin P. Ansley's mansion on The Prado. Ansley's home would later become the Georgia governor's mansion.

The Tudor-style, two-story residence of J.O. Wynn and his wife, Adelaide, located at 1126 Peachtree Street (since demolished), is shown in this c. 1908 photograph. Despite the horse-drawn carriage parked under the porte cochere, transportation changes were taking place. Ansley Park was designed for driving. In the July 8, 1906, issue of the *Atlanta Constitution*, the suburb was lauded as "the future social and driving center of Atlanta."

Born in Alabama in 1857, Porter King graduated in 1878 from Howard College and studied law at the University of Virginia. In 1882, he moved to Atlanta to practice law and quickly became established. In 1889, he was elected to the city council, and in 1894, against light opposition, he was elected the 34th mayor of Atlanta, serving from 1895 to 1897. He was also on the board of directors of the 1895 Cotton States and International Exposition held in Piedmont Park. Elected to the Georgia General Assembly in 1900, health problems forced him to resign after only a week in office. In 1901, he died at his home on Merritts Avenue. Subsequently, his widow, Carrie King, moved to the house shown in the c. 1908 photograph below. This home, since demolished, was located on Peachtree Street near Seventeenth Street.

Enos S. Hartman was the proprietor of a haberdashery located at 6 Peachtree Street. The Atlanta city directory of 1914–1915 indicates that his merchandise included shoes, hats, and furnishings. In 1908–1909, he and his wife, Carrie G. Hartman, resided in this two-story house, since demolished, on Lafayette Drive. It was one of the first houses built on the street.

According to Rick Beard, advertisements for the September 15, 1905, auction "listed the names of prominent Atlantans who were soon expected to begin construction in the development. Among the prospective residents were George Nobel and Frank McRae, two prominent physicians." The above photograph, taken around 1908, is of Dr. Nobel's house, then located at 980 Peachtree Street. The house was constructed at a cost of $15,000. It has since been demolished.

The c. 1908 photograph above shows the home of lawyer and capitalist Charles J. Haden. It was located on Peachtree Street near Le Reve, the home of A.G. Rhodes. The home has since been demolished. In the photograph below, taken sometime between 1937 and 1941, Haden (right) and Governor Rivers (left) dedicate a plaque at the summit of Brasstown Bald, the highest mountain in Georgia. The plaque has since been removed. According to historian Franklin M. Garrett, in 1919, Haden was an unwitting participant in a cruel hoax. While sitting on a stage in Atlanta with Vice Pres. Thomas Marshall, who was about to deliver a speech, Haden was handed a message that President Wilson had died. Haden told Marshall and then announced the sad news to the audience. Marshall asked everyone to pray for him and left the stage. The message was false.

In 1945, Charles and Margaret Pittman lived at 130 The Prado. In this photograph from around 1939, probably taken in the backyard of their previous residence at 1886 Monroe Drive, the Pittmans' daughter Ann stands between her playpen and Bill Lyons Jr., who lived next door. Tallulah Ellis Reed (now Mrs. William Lyons) lived at 1793 Flagler Avenue (the Ansley Annex) and was Ann's classmate at both Spring Street and Westminster Schools. (Courtesy of William Lyons.)

This house, located at 34 Peachtree Circle (now 96 Peachtree Circle), was one of the first built on Peachtree Circle. It is seen here around 1908. The lot was purchased for $825 at the auction on June 19, 1906 (40 lots were sold that day for $41,160). In 1912, the improved property had an assessed value of $4,000. It was the residence of attorney J.H. Pitman and his wife, Elizabeth. His law office was located at 218 Kiser Building. Based on data compiled by Rick Beard, the average cost of the 24 two-story houses built in Ansley Park between 1906 and 1908 was about $8,200.

David H. Gambrell, who lived in Ansely Park for 15 years, has had a remarkably distinguished career. In 1963, he founded the Atlanta law firm of Gambrell & Stoltz. Subsequently, he served as the president of the Atlanta Bar Association (1965–1966) and as president of the State Bar Association (1967–1968). He is the recipient of the State Bar Association's Distinguished Service Award, the Atlanta Bar Association's Leadership Award, and the Fellows of the American Bar Association's Distinguished Service Award. From 1970 to 1971, he was the chairman of the Georgia Democratic Party. When long-serving US Senator Richard Russell Jr. died in office, Gov. Jimmy Carter appointed Gambrell to the US Senate, a position he held from 1971 to 1972. Gambrell has since served on, or chaired, a number of boards and committees and remains senior counsel at the successor of the law firm he founded. This 1970s photograph of Senator Gambrell was taken in front of the Russell Senate Office Building in Washington, DC. (Courtesy of David H. Gambrell.)

In the photograph at right, taken around 1936, future US Senator David Gambrell (left) and his brother Bobby stand on the driveway of their residence at 5 Ansley Drive. This is a short street that was then adjacent to the governor's mansion. The 2012 photograph below shows the house as it now appears, with the front porch enclosed. (Right, courtesy of David Gambrell; below, author's collection.)

According to Rick Beard, the slowdown in construction in Atlanta during World War I resulted in a 10-year housing shortage. When construction activity in Ansley picked up in 1919, the focus was no longer on building single-family residences. "Apartment buildings, most of which were built on the periphery of the suburb, were being built in great numbers. Twenty-two of the thirty-two apartment buildings ever constructed appeared between 1919 and 1929." The above photograph, taken in the 1920s, is of the apartment house located at 18 Peachtree Circle. It is now the Peachtree Circle Condominiums. Below, the Grafton Apartments, now a condominium located at 3 Park Lane, are pictured in the 1940s or 1950s. This building, constructed in 1935, was designed by architect Ten Eyck Brown. (Below, courtesy of Special Collections and Archives, Georgia State University.)

The 1920s Neo-Palladian Italian Villa Apartments, completed in 1926, are located next to the Ansley Golf Club at 200 Montgomery Ferry Drive. This is now The Villa, a condominium. It was designed by Hentz, Reid & Adler sometime between 1923 and 1926, when Neel Reid was the firm's head designer. Asa Griggs Chandler Jr., the second son of the Coca-Cola tycoon, and Martin Dunbar led the developers.

The two-story frame residence of R.R. Wood at 22 Fifteenth Street (later 156 Fifteenth Street) is seen here around 1908. The home has since been demolished. The construction permit issued on May 10, 1907, indicates an estimated cost of $8,000. A number of chickens can be seen in the front yard.

In 1908–1909, Edward L. Bishop and his wife, Phoebe Prioleau Ellis Bishop, lived at 115 East Fifteenth Street (now 229 East Fifteenth Street), seen above. Edward was a cashier at the Phenix Mutual Fire Insurance Company. The Bishops subsequently moved to 96 Westminster Drive. Mrs. Edgar J. Forio Jr. (previously Phoebe Ellis Gould) remembers that she liked to visit her great aunt because she could also visit the cow named Moomoo kept in the back yard. Phoebe Bishop liked to have fresh milk and cream, and so her "driver" would milk the cow. This Westminster residence was later demolished and replaced with a modern house. The left photograph, taken around 1915, shows Phoebe wearing a stovepipe hat. The setting is probably in front of the home of Fay Pearce's great-grandfather, Judge William D. Ellis, located at 49 Eleventh Street. (Left, courtesy of E. Fay Pearce Jr.)

In 1939, family and friends gathered in the side yard of the Pearce home at 339 Beverly Road. The occasion was the baptism of Edmund Fay Pearce Jr. Those standing are, from left to right, Phoebe Ellis Gould, Sue Boyd, P.W. Smith, E. Fay Pearce Sr. (holding Fay Jr.), Annie Stuart Pearce (Fay Jr.'s mother), F. Stuart Gould Jr., and Sarah Smith. The children in the front are Stuart and Phoebe Gould. The house in the background, located at 30 Polo Drive, was the home of artist Louis Gregg. Below, Fay Pearce Sr. readies a showerhead at his backyard canvas pool on Beverly Road around 1941. Sitting in the pool waiting to be sprayed are, from left to right, Fay Jr., Stuart Gould, Phoebe Gould, Gail Whitaker, and Stella Pearce. (Courtesy of E. Fay Pearce Jr.)

Fay Pearce Jr., in a beret, coat, and gloves, plays with his toy truck and crane near the front steps of the family home on Beverly Road around 1941. Behind him can be seen many a boy's favorite toy, a pedal car. Fay graduated in 1960 from Georgia Tech and had a successful 33-year career with the Coca-Cola Company. (Courtesy of E. Fay Pearce Jr.)

This 1940s photograph is of Phoebe Prioleau Ellis Bishop (right) and her namesake, Phoebe Ellis Gould (now Mrs. Edgar J. Forio Jr.). They are sitting in the yard of the Bishop home on Westminster Drive. There are at least 30 descendants in the Prioleau and Ellis families with the given name of Phoebe. (Courtesy of E. Fay Pearce Jr.)

Plat of
Ansley Park Annex
land lots 56 & 57-17th Dist. of Fulton Co.
O.F. Kauffman & Bro. Civ. Eng'rs.
June 1913

The Ansley Annex was Edwin Ansley's last attempt at developing the subdivision. As seen on this 1913 plat, the annex was a rectangular-shaped development with North Boulevard (later renamed Monroe Drive) and the Ansley Park Golf Links on its long sides and Montgomery Ferry Drive (at that time not connected to the boulevard) and Rock Springs Avenue on its short sides. The majority of the lots were on Flagler Avenue. Rick Beard noted that "when compared with those of the suburb proper, these lots were on all counts an embarrassment and no amount of puffery could conceal that fact." Consequently, of the 25 lots offered at the 1913 auction, only five were sold.

The above photograph shows the house at 1793 Flagler Avenue, the residence of the Reed family, in the 1940s. On each side of the house can be seen a neighboring structure: a house on the left and a garage on the right. Houses on Flagler were built very close together. Other than modifications to the landscaping, the appearance of this house has changed little since the 1940s. Shown below around 1944, sitting on their backdoor steps, are Tallulah and Fred with their daughters Tallulah (center) and Betty (right). Fred, wearing his Army uniform, was called into service in his mid-30s and arrived at the Battle of the Bulge just before the Germans attacked in December 1944. After the war, he owned and successfully operated Fred Reed Picture Framing. (Courtesy of Tallulah Reed Lyons.)

In this 1940s photograph, one of the Reed sisters sits on the sidewalk at the bottom of their driveway on what appears to be an unpaved Flagler Drive. In the background, cars are parked at the curb on both sides of the street and a man cuts grass with a push lawnmower while a child appears to follow along in a pedal car. (Courtesy of Tallulah Reed Lyons.)

While their house on Flagler was under construction, the Reeds lived in a backyard cabin. In this c. 1941 photograph, taken in front of that still-standing cabin, Flagler children, watched over by three maids, enjoy a neighborhood party. Tallulah Reed is held in place by the maid on the right. Other children include Caroline Cole, Tommy Moore, Nina Hopkins, Stanley Ray, and Bill Bivens. (Courtesy of Tallulah Reed Lyons.)

Tallulah Reed, seen here around 1942, stands on the front porch of her Flagler home. She is holding, with the aid of a knee, her much-loved dog Socky. Her sister Betty stands at the other end of the porch. The neighboring house is visible behind Betty. (Courtesy of Tallulah Reed Lyons.)

Six Ansley Park toddlers, sitting on a joggling board with their mothers standing behind them, posed for this photograph in the 1930s. The likely location of this gathering is the Ansley Park home of Tallulah Reed's grandmother Codington, who lived at 67 Avery Drive. (Courtesy of Tallulah Reed Lyons.)

Five

MARGARET MITCHELL

Margaret Munnerlyn "Peggy" Mitchell, seen here around 1936, lived a large part of her life in or around Ansley Park. Born in Atlanta on November 8, 1900, she grew up hearing firsthand accounts of the Civil War from veterans, one of whom was her paternal grandfather, Russell Crawford Mitchell. Margaret attended the Tenth Street School, Woodberry Hall, the Washington Seminary, and spent one year at Smith College. From 1922 to 1926, she worked as a reporter for the *Atlanta Journal Sunday Magazine*. In 1925, she married John Marsh. Her first and only published novel, *Gone With the Wind*, a love story set in the midst of the Civil War and Reconstruction, won the 1937 Pulitzer Prize for fiction and became a phenomenal best seller. The movie adaptation of the book, which premiered at the Loews Grand Theater in Atlanta on December 15, 1939, won 10 Academy Awards and is considered by many to be one of the best films of all time. On August 11, 1949, while crossing Peachtree Street on the way to a movie theater, Margaret Mitchell was hit by a drunk driver. She died several days later.

In 1912, Margaret's father, Eugene Mitchell, a real estate attorney, moved his family into a Classical Revival mansion located on Peachtree Street (later 1401 Peachtree Street), which was at that time a part of Ansley Park. The property, purchased in 1909, had an assessed value in 1912 of $12,000. In this photograph from around 1930, Margaret and her dad look at a book while seated next to a Doric column at the front of the house. The house was demolished in the 1950s.

This c. 1935 photograph shows Margaret Mitchell working on a sewing table with a portable typewriter. She worked in a similar setting in the front room of the Marsh apartment at 17 Crescent Avenue. Missing from this scene is the eyeshade she always wore while typing. It was in this tiny apartment, which Margaret called "The Dump," that most of *Gone With the Wind* was written.

In 1935, Harold Latham, an editor-in-chief at MacMillan Company, embarked on a scouting trip for new fiction. In Atlanta, his first stop, he made what proved to be the discovery of a lifetime: the previously unread (except by John Marsh) manuscript of *Gone With the Wind*. On August 6, MacMillan signed a contract with Mitchell. In this posed photograph from around 1937, Latham and Mitchell examine a document.

A few months before the premier of *Gone With the Wind*, the Marshes moved to Ansley Park. Their new home was in the Della Manta Apartments at 1268 Piedmont Avenue. This apartment house (now One South Prado, a condominium) is located across the street from the Piedmont Driving Club. Designed in 1917 by architect Neel Reid, it is listed in the National Register of Historic Places. (Author's collection.)

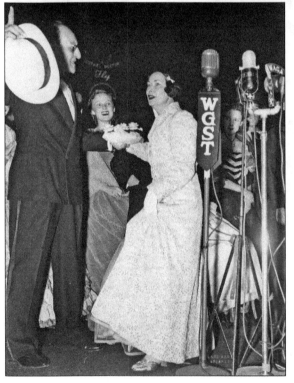

On December 14, 1939, Rich's Department Store held a luncheon for Margaret. According to biographer Finis Farr, "someone pulled back a chair just as the guest of honor was about to sit in it. Miss Mitchell took a fall that jarred her spine." The next day, still in pain, Mitchell walked across the street to attend a tea party held at the Piedmont Driving Club. Shown above are, from left to right, Vivien Leigh (Scarlet O'Hara), Clark Gable (Rhett Butler), Margaret Mitchell, and David O. Selznick, the film's producer. The left photograph shows Mitchell arriving at the Loews Grand Theater. She is greeted on the stage by master of ceremonies Julian Boehm, who, Farr reports, greeted her with "God bless little Peggy Marsh"—she was a petite lady of four feet, eleven inches.

On premiere night, the Loews Grand Theater, which had seats for about 2,000 people, was packed with notables that included Bobby Jones (second row, second from the left). Robert Tyre Jones Jr., a native of Atlanta and an attorney, was a great American athlete. In 1930, he completed a grand slam of golf by winning all four of the major championships.

Shown at the premier of *Gone With the Wind* are, from left to right, an unidentified lady (possibly Olivia de Havilland), John Hay Whitney, Margaret Mitchell, and John Marsh. Whitney inherited a fortune. During his lifetime, he published the *New York Herald Tribune*, served as US ambassador to the United Kingdom, and invested in Broadway shows and movies. His position as chairman of the Selnick Production Company probably gained him the coveted seat next to the author.

In this c. 1945 photograph, taken in the Marshes' Ansley Park apartment, Margaret Mitchell is shown looking at one of the many letters she regularly received. According to biographer Anne Edwards, writing in *Road to Tara: The Life of Margaret Mitchell*, "she managed to [personally] answer about a hundred letters a week."

After settling Mitchell's estate and, as she directed, burning her correspondence, John Marsh moved from Della Manta to 26 Walker Terrace, an Ansley Park bungalow a mere stone's throw from the apartment. This photograph shows the Walker Terrace house as it appeared in 2012. Marsh died on May 5, 1952, less than three years after his wife's tragic death. (Author's collection.)

Six

SOCIAL ORGANIZATIONS

Since its founding in 1887 as a prestigious social club devoted to the driving of horse-drawn carriages, the Piedmont Driving Club has been the meeting place of Atlanta's elite. Much of the club's premises, originally composed of 190 acres of land purchased from Benjamin "Doc" Walker, were leased to the city of Atlanta for the 1887 and 1895 Expositions. The land, which now includes Piedmont Park, was purchased by the city in 1904. This postcard image from the 1880s or 1890s shows a number of occupants of horse-drawn vehicles at the side of the Walker home, which was originally used as the clubhouse. (Author's collection.)

Fifteenth Street, one of the first streets constructed in Ansley Park, linked Peachtree Street to the Piedmont Driving Club. According to Rick Beard, Edwin Ansley's plan was to provide "a pleasure driving area for the city's most prominent citizens. In March 1906 he offered to trade fifty acres of land in the suburb for the Piedmont Driving Club's five acres in Piedmont Park if the Club would move to the new site." The members decided not to accept the offer (perhaps due to their expectation of a 1910 International Exposition) but to expand the buildings in their current location. The above photograph, taken around 1902, shows the clubhouse (left) and the New York Building, built for the 1895 Exposition and subsequently used by the club. The rotogravure photograph below, from around 1915, shows the front of the club as seen from the Piedmont Avenue entrance.

On December 7, 1902, James W. English, Civil War captain, banker, and mayor of Atlanta from 1881 to 1883, gave a reception at the Piedmont Driving Club for Gov. Joseph M. Terrell (1861–1912). In addition to serving two terms as governor, Terrell also served Georgia as its attorney general for five terms and as a US senator. This photograph of guests at the reception was taken in the New York Building.

Guests attending a formal ball at the Piedmont Driving Club are shown in this c. 1910 photograph. Note the orchestra and servers visible in the background.

This c. 1910 photograph is of a banquet at the Piedmont Driving Club. According to the Atlanta History Center's caption, the occasion for the banquet was "possibly the visit of President William Howard Taft." Taft was the 27th president (1909–1913) and the 10th chief justice of the United States (1921–1930).

A group of impeccably dressed ladies attend a luncheon at the Piedmont Driving Club in 1910.

The Nine O'Clocks is a social organization of young eligible bachelors. Founded in 1883, it is the oldest bachelor's club in Atlanta. The members have been partying twice a year for 130 years. Here, members gather at a costume ball held at the Piedmont Driving Club around 1925.

In 1948, the Atlanta Debutante Club held its Halloween Ball at the Piedmont Driving Club. According to the Georgia Archives caption, "the debutantes were presented, after which dinner was served and a dance held." This photograph was taken at the dinner. (Courtesy of the Georgia Archives, Vanishing Georgia Collection, ful0079.)

The Coca-Cola Company, headquartered in Atlanta, was for 50 years led by Robert W. Woodruff. After his father and a group of investors purchased the company in 1919, it initially experienced financial problems. The son took over as president in 1923 and turned the company into a financial success and one of the world's best-known brands. Above, Woodruff (far right) is shown with unidentified guests at a Piedmont Driving Company party in 1951. The below photograph, from around 1950, is a view of the club from Piedmont Avenue.

In 1896, the Piedmont Driving Club built Atlanta's first, though short-lived, golf course on land that would become Piedmont Park. By the early 1900s, golf had grown in popularity. National enthusiasm for the sport took hold in 1913 when Francis Quimet, an American amateur, won the US Open by defeating two of Britain's top players. With golf confirmed as a real estate amenity, Edwin P. Ansley proceeded with constructing a nine-hole course and also proposed building tennis courts, a polo field, and a swimming pool on land less desirable for home construction. The image above is from the February 11, 1913, *Atlanta Journal Newspaper.* It shows Ansley (third from left) and a group of unidentified men reviewing plans for the development. At right, a drawing of the Ansley Park streets includes at top right one of the early course designs. (Both, courtesy of Ansley Golf Club.)

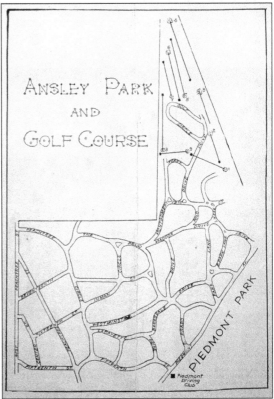

The first permanent 18-hole course, the Atlanta Athletic Club's Eastlake, was completed in 1908. Within four years, courses were constructed or planned in Druid Hills, Brookhaven, and Ansley Park. At a cost of about $100,000, the Ansley Park golf links, "designed for the average golfer," was laid out in 1912 and completed the following year. Above, an image from a 1913 advertising brochure shows Edwin P. Ansley with a prospective member on the newly developed course. They are standing beside Ansley's 1911 Pierce-Arrow, a luxury automobile of the era. The below photograph, taken around 1914, is of the Jones family, golf pro Willie McKenzie, and three caddies (two partially visible in the background) taking refreshments while on a golf outing at the Ansley links. (Both, courtesy of Ansley Golf Club.)

Ansley's master plan for the links originally included an imposing clubhouse designed by acclaimed architect W.L. Stoddard. With the onset in 1914 of World War I, Ansley's financial condition deteriorated. Due to dissatisfaction with escalating greens fees, a group of players formed the Ansley Park Golf Club, which was incorporated on March 15, 1915. The corporation negotiated a $150 per month rental of the links and gained permission to build a clubhouse. The structure they built, at a cost of $1,000, was a modest one-story wood-framed "house" with a 480-square-foot living room, locker rooms, showers, workshop, and office. The drawing to the right is of the planned two-story clubhouse. Below, a c. 1915 photograph shows the clubhouse as it was actually built and used for 13 years. (Both, courtesy of Ansley Golf Club.)

G.C. "Billy" Jones (left) is pictured in the 1920s. In 1922, when he was only 16, Jones became the first recorded Ansley Golf Club (AGC) champion. In 1946, comedian Bob Hope played an exhibition match at the Ansley Park Golf Club with Louise Suggs, the founder of the Ladies Professional Golf Association and a member of the World Golf Hall of Fame. Below, Hope is shown making a shot in the rough of a Clear Creek tributary. Watching from the creek bank are, from left to right, Suggs, amateur champion Dorothy Kirby, and Lt. Col. T.S. Rawlings. (Left, courtesy of Ansley Golf Club; below, courtesy of Bob Hope Enterprises.)

AGC's first pool, which had to be drained each week for cleaning, wasn't built until around 1934. A regulation short course pool was constructed in the 1950s. Early Ansley swimmers were strong competitors in the Havalanta Games, an annual competition held from 1948 to 1959 between Havana, Cuba, and Atlanta. Above, the Atlanta team is gathered in Havana around 1951. Ansley team members included Art Benton (first row, third from left); Todd Dwyer, AGC president from 1978 to 1979 (between the first row and second row, far right); and Sandy Benton and Gail Benton (third row, second and third from left, respectively). Below, Sandra Benton Pearce (far left) and other swimmers are seen at the pool in 1948. (Both, courtesy of Art Benton.)

The clubhouse entrance on Montgomery Ferry Drive is seen here in the 1950s. (Courtesy of Ansley Golf Club.)

Groundbreaking ceremonies for the tennis pavilion which was later named in honor of then-president Bill Walton (pictured here removing the first spade of dirt).

Tennis came to the AGC in 1964 when three courts were constructed. In 1970, the first full-time tennis professional, Dale Leprevost, was hired. By 1974, three more courts had been added. Bill Walton, club president from 1972 to 1976, was the impetus behind construction of the tennis pavilion, which opened in 1976. Here, Walton removes the first spade of dirt at the ground-breaking ceremony. (Courtesy of Ansley Golf Club.)

82

A long-time AGC member recalled that Ansley was joined by those who "wanted to have a good time." "And Ansley," club historian David Swann recounts, "knew how to have a good time. There were numerous social events—summer opening, the New Year's Eve Ball, the President's Ball, and the fall dinner dance." The above photograph, taken in the AGC living room during the 1977 President's Ball, shows Robert Robinette, club general manager from 1972 to 1978 (left) and Frank Sinatra Jr., a singer, songwriter, and conductor, and son of actor and singer Frank Sinatra and Nancy Barbato. The 1970s advertising brochure image below shows an unidentified couple at the clubhouse entrance. (Both, courtesy of Ansley Golf Club.)

The side and rear of the "old" clubhouse are seen here in the 1970s. On the right, a player is shown putting on the No. 9 green. (Courtesy of Ansley Golf Club.)

The caption to this 1970s advertising brochure image reads: "firm, fresh greens, plus a challenging layout, make the Ansley course appealing to all types of golfers. Twin tees double the use of each green, turning the course into an 18-hole in-town play." In 1999, when the club merged with Settindown Creek Golf Club, Ansley members gained a second clubhouse and a nationally ranked 18-hole course. (Courtesy of Ansley Golf Club.)

Ansley Park residents were well represented in the leading women's organizations, such as the Daughters of the American Revolution (DAR) and the United Daughters of the Confederacy. In 1920, according to Rick Beard, about 19 percent of the Atlanta members of these two women's organizations resided in Ansley Park. This c. 1910 photograph shows Lucy Cook Peel in costume as Mrs. Malaprop in *The Rivals*, a play by Richard Sheridan. The founder of the Joseph Habersham Chapter of the DAR, Lucy was the daughter of Confederate General Philip Cook, who, during the course of the Civil War, advanced in rank from private to brigadier general. A graduate of Oglethorpe University and the University of Virginia, he subsequently practiced law in Americus, Georgia, and represented the state in the US House of Representatives from 1873 until 1883.

The Craigie House, shown in the 1920s postcard image above, is the former home of the Atlanta chapter of the Daughters of the American Revolution. Organized in 1891, this chapter is the nation's second oldest. Located at 1204 Piedmont Avenue (a short distance from the Piedmont Driving Club), the Craigie House, built in 1911, is named after the Massachusetts home of poet Henry Wadsworth Longfellow. Habersham Memorial Hall (shown below in the 1960s), located in Ansley Park at 270 Fifteenth Street, was previously the home of the Joseph Habersham chapter of the DAR. Erected in 1922, this beautiful Federal Revival building was designed by architect Henry Hornbostel, who, according to *Ansley Park: 100 Years of Gracious Living*, "also designed . . . Callanwolde, which was a large Tudor Revival mansion built for the Candler family of Atlanta's Coca-Cola fortune." The building is now condominiums. (Above, author's collection.)

Seven

HOUSES OF WORSHIP

First Church of Christ, Scientist, seen here in an undated photograph, is a well-recognized downtown Atlanta landmark. This beautiful church is located at the Peachtree Street and Fifteenth Street entrance to Ansley Park. Homes on Peachtree Circle and around Winn Park are visible in the background. This church was informally begun in Sue Harper Mims's residence at 575 Peachtree Street, at the corner of Peachtree Street and Ponce de Leon. That address is now the location of the Georgia Terrace Hotel. When the congregation outgrew its first church on Baker Street, the membership decided to move to its present Ansley Park location. As described by church historians, some of the outstanding features of this structure, completed in 1914 at a cost of $87,272, include its "neo-classical or Greek revival style . . . the intricate brickwork and masonry of the exterior walls of the building . . . six columns with Corinthian capitals . . . six paneled doors, measuring almost 14 feet in height, [and a copper] . . . dome which stands 100 feet above the ground floor." (Courtesy of First Church of Christ, Scientist.)

The establishment of the Christian Science church in Atlanta (the first Christian Science church in the South) grew directly out of the healing work of Mary Baker Eddy and her students. According to church tradition, in the late 1880s, Sue Harper Mims, shown in this undated photograph, was healed of a long-term affliction by one of Eddy's students, Julia S. Bartlett, a Christian Science lecturer and practitioner. Mims had suffered for 15 years from a painful illness that prevented her from walking more than a few blocks. After listening to a lecture given by Bartlett, Mims requested Christian Science treatment from her. Mims soon experienced relief from her longstanding physical problems and enthusiastically took up the study of Eddy's book *Science and Health with Key to the Scriptures* (the "textbook" of Christian Science), which is inspired by the Bible. Mims subsequently became a nationally recognized Christian Science practitioner and lecturer. It was her devotion that led, in 1893, to the founding of First Church of Christ, Scientist, in Atlanta. (Courtesy of First Church of Christ, Scientist.)

The c. 1910 photograph above is of Sue Harper Mims's Ansley Park home on Peachtree Circle, where she moved after the death of her husband, Maj. Livingston Mims. He is seen in the undated photograph at right. Before the Civil War, Major Mims had been a businessman and a member of the Mississippi legislature. During the war, he fought in several campaigns and served on the staff of Gen. Joseph Johnston. Afterward, he was the Atlanta manager of the New York Life Insurance Company. In October 1900, he was elected mayor of Atlanta. (Courtesy of First Church of Christ, Scientist.)

Arthur Neal Robinson Sr. designed the Peachtree Street home of the First Church of Christ, Scientist, of which he was a member. He received his architectural training at the University of Georgia and was an apprentice of architect Edward E. Daugherty, who had trained at the Ecole des Beaux-Arts. Robinson and his wife, the former Flossie Japp of Cincinnati, are seen here in the 1920s. (Courtesy of First Church of Christ, Scientist.)

Daisy Arnold Eastman sits with a dog on her lap in front of First Church of Christ, Scientist in the 1920s. The photograph was taken at the fountain located at the intersection of Peachtree Circle and Fifteenth Street, which is now the home of the Trilon, designed by Atlanta artist Steffen Thomas. The fountain was erected in 1916 by Mrs. Joseph Madison High, DAR regent and patron of the arts.

The Peachtree Circle home of J.S. Barbour is seen here around 1908. Barbour was identified in the Atlanta city directory as the assistant to the president of the Southern Railroad. A woman is visible in the window on the second floor. According to *Ansley Park: 100 Years of Gracious Living*, this structure "was originally the home of Henry G. Kohrt and designed by Fox Theatre architect P. Thornton Marye." Located next to First Church of Christ, Scientist, the house was acquired by the church and now serves as its reading room and nursery.

At the first service in the building on Baker Street, Sue Harper Mims served as first reader and Edward R. Carman as second reader. In 1907, Carman, living at 43 Peachtree Circle, was Mims's next-door-neighbor. The Atlanta city directory of 1907 lists Carman as a Christian Scientist practitioner with an office at 529 Candler Building.

Peachtree Christian Church, seen above in the 1950s, is located at 1580 Peachtree Street, a short distance from Rhodes Hall and Peachtree Circle. After completing only the foundation and assembly room, the church ran out of money. A.G. Rhodes, a member of the church, donated the funds for the sanctuary. The church was dedicated in October 1928. As designed by the architect Charles H. Hopson, the sanctuary and main building are expressions of Gothic 15th-century English architecture. The Annie Laurie Warren Chapel, located adjacent to the narthex of the sanctuary, was built in 1949. Dr. L.O. Bricker, the founding minister, served as the active minister until 1930. Below, Dr. Bricker, his wife, Nee Acker, and daughter, Eileen, pose in the 1920s. He subsequently married Louanna Rhodes, the daughter of A.G. Rhodes. (Both, courtesy of Peachtree Christian Church.)

The Peachtree Christian Church choir sang antiphonally from a loft above the altar and from the balcony. The 1938 Easter service photograph above shows them surrounding the altar and in front of the baptistery painting. The Fellowship Hall was used for many church functions. Below is a dinner in the hall on February 22, 1939. The hall, later named for active elder Stew Wood, is now used for receptions, concerts, seminars, and other events. (Both, courtesy of Peachtree Christian Church.)

The two-story-high Peachtree Christian Church auditorium, which was completed in 1925, had theater seating for over 300. This area is now used for children's education and by Peachtree Childtown, the church's early-learning center. Above, the Vanguard class is shown sitting in the auditorium around 1926. The lady in the front row, Mrs. Frank Mason Robinson, was likely the class pianist. Her husband was one of the originators of the Coca-Cola logo. The below photograph was taken at the men's retreat at Camp Ko-Wee-Ta on June 5, 1948. Wearing a dress shirt and tie, Dr. Burns, who became the active minister in 1930, is seated in the boat holding a fishing pole. The two men standing on the dock and facing the camera are Max Gokee (left) and Charles McLaughlin. (Both, courtesy of Peachtree Christian Church.)

At right, Dr. Robert W. Burns, active minister from 1930 to 1970, holds hands with Dewey and Rosemary Hardy at a Wedding Bells Service around 1940. This annual service, in which couples renew their wedding vows, is a Peachtree Christian tradition and is now observed on St. Valentine's Sunday. With its medieval-styled cathedral and beautiful stained-glass windows, this church is a popular location for weddings—over 8,800 have been held there. Below, Dr. Burns, in a sanctuary tour on April 3, 1960, leads young children behind the altar to view the baptistery. (Both, courtesy of Peachtree Christian Church.)

The sanctuary of the Peachtree Christian Church features 12 major English stained-glass windows. In the view of the sanctuary above, during a service in 1961, some of the 10 side windows are partially visible. In addition, The Jesus Christ is Lord Window, indistinctly seen above the back gallery, shows Christ with outstretched hands in a welcoming gesture flanked by various historic church leaders. The Great Commission Window, located above the front gallery, not visible, depicts the risen Christ's ascension to heaven. In the below photograph from around 1948, Dr. Burns (left) and attorney Elbert Tuttle, a future judge for the US Court of Appeals, perform a ground-breaking ceremony for the Annie Laurie Warren Chapel. This chapel was funded by Commodore and Mrs. Virgil P. Warren and dedicated in honor of Annie Warren in October 1949. (Both, courtesy of Peachtree Christian Church.)

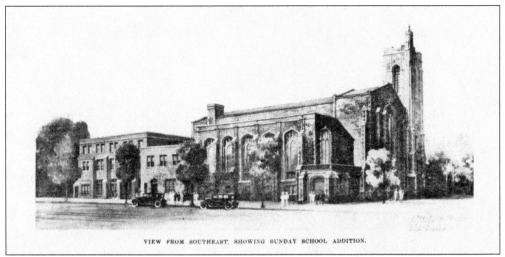

VIEW FROM SOUTHEAST, SHOWING SUNDAY SCHOOL ADDITION.

The First Presbyterian Church of Atlanta, founded in 1848, was initially located on Marietta Street. Seeking to escape downtown commercial development, the church purchased a suburban lot from church elder S.M. Inman, a cotton magnate. On December 5, 1915, Dr. J. Sprole Lyons preached the first sermon in the newly constructed Sunday school building, located at Peachtree and Sixteenth Streets. The English Gothic sanctuary was completed in 1919. In 1929, the Sunday school building was expanded and the bell tower completed. Edwin P. Ansley, the developer of Ansley Park, served as a church deacon from 1912 until his death in 1923. An architectural drawing from the 1920s (above) shows a Sixteenth Street view of the church with the planned Sunday school expansion. The below photograph from the 1930s shows a Peachtree Street view of the front of the church. (Both, courtesy of First Presbyterian Church of Atlanta.)

Dr. J. Sprole Lyons, seen at left around 1919, received his religious education at King College and Union Theological Seminary. After serving in Louisville, Kentucky, for 22 years, Dr. Lyons pastored the First Presbyterian Church of Atlanta from 1914 until his retirement in 1936. It was under his leadership that the church moved to its current Peachtree Street location. According to church historian and elder George B. Hoyt, Dr. Lyons "was very meticulous in dress and manner, preached strong exegetical sermons, and had a great gift as an organizer." Arlene Peffer, shown below in the 1920s, was renowned for her faultless memory. For many years, she served as Dr. Lyons's devoted secretary. According to church historians Beth Dawkins Bassett and Gayle White, Peffer was "a tireless worker in the mission activities of First Church." (Both, courtesy of First Presbyterian Church of Atlanta.)

The following special message was written on this Sunday school photograph: "Cradle Club Class, First Presbyterian Church send love, Mother's Day, May 10, 1925." Only one of these children is identified: Eleanor Hoyt (now Eleanor Dabney) is the girl at the far right. (Courtesy of First Presbyterian Church of Atlanta.)

This photograph shows unidentified children attending the Daily Vacation Bible School at First Presbyterian Church of Atlanta from June 11 through July 6, 1928. Except for the two children sitting at the bottom right (who are probably just clowning for the camera), the group seems to be enjoying a day at camp. (Courtesy of First Presbyterian Church of Atlanta.)

Church historians Ruth Dawkins Bassett and Gayle White indicate that "in 1922, the Atlanta Presbytery began holding conferences for children, youth, and adults at Camp Smyrna." The above photograph, taken in the 1940s, shows Dr. Gardner (far left) sitting on a porch swing at the camp with, from left to right, Fraser Hart, Benn Dunn, Jane Jones, and Billy Parigna. Dr. William V. Gardner pastored the church from 1936 to 1952. He earned both his bachelor's and master's degrees in divinity from Union Theological Seminary and his doctorate in theology from Presbyterian College. Dr. Gardner saw the church through the difficult years of World War II. At left, Camp Smyrna Youth Conference attendees Dorothy Ragsdale (left) and Betty King stand in front of a camp cabin in the 1940s. (Both, courtesy of First Presbyterian Church of Atlanta.)

The Temple on Peachtree Street (pictured) is the third permanent place of worship of the Hebrew Benevolent Congregation of Atlanta. While a Jewish community existed in Atlanta as early as the 1840s, the Hebrew Benevolent Society did not incorporate until 1861. Its first synagogue was located at the corner of Forsyth and Garnett Streets. The Moorish building was dedicated on August 31, 1877, by the congregation's new rabbi, Dr. Edward Benjamin Morris Browne. A man of many accomplishments, Browne held several European degrees, earned medical and law degrees in America, was a medical school professor, a newspaper editor, and a Talmud expert. In need of more space, the congregation moved in 1902 to its second house of worship, at the corner of South Pryor and Richardson Streets. The third move was to its current location, across from the Peachtree Christian Church and near Ansley Park. Rabbi David Marx dedicated The Temple in June 1931. (Courtesy of The Breman Jewish Heritage Museum.)

In 1895, 23-year-old David Marx, only a year out of rabbinical school, became the seventh rabbi to serve the Hebrew Benevolent Congregation. He held that position until 1946. In describing Marx's leadership challenges during the more than 50 years of his tenure, Temple historian Janice Rothschild-Blumberg noted that he led the congregation "through the miseries of the most violent strife in the city's history, one of the worst incidents of anti-Semitism in the nation's history, and the two most terrible wars in world history." His theological leadership included acting as the peacemaker in restoring harmonious relations when the majority vote was for adopting Reform Judaism. Marx is seen at left in the early 1900s as a young rabbi. Below, Rabbi Marx is seen in The Temple pulpit in the 1940s. (Both, courtesy of The Breman Jewish Heritage Museum.)

These photographs are of the first confirmation and wedding held at the newly constructed temple on Peachtree Street. The above photograph, taken on the front steps of The Temple, is of the 1931 confirmation class of 15 men and 10 women. Below is the 1931 wedding party of Dorothy Selig and Lyons B. Joel. The matron of honor, to the groom's right, is his sister, Josephine Joel Heyman. (Both, courtesy of The Breman Jewish Heritage Museum.)

Jacob M. Rothschild, shown speaking from the pulpit in the 1950s, was the eighth rabbi to serve the Hebrew Benevolent Congregation of Atlanta and only the second to serve at The Temple on Peachtree Street. He held this position from 1946 until 1973. During this period, Rothschild ably led the congregation through a period of growth and turbulent social changes. (Courtesy of The Breman Jewish Heritage Museum.)

On October 12, 1958, The Temple was bombed. According to historian Janice Rothschild-Blumberg, "some members suspected that Rabbi Rothschild had brought this [about] . . . by his outspoken defense of human rights for the Negro." No one was ever convicted, though five men were accused of the bombing. In this photograph, taken at the north side entrance where the dynamite was set, two men, probably Atlanta police detectives, stand in front of the 20-foot hole caused by the explosion. (Courtesy of The Breman Jewish Heritage Museum.)

Eight

SCHOOLS

Rosa Louise Woodberry graduated from the Houghton Institute in Augusta and from the Lucy Cobb Institute in Athens. After initially denied admission to the University of Georgia, she became the first female admitted to that institution. In 1927 she received a bachelor's degree from the University of Georgia, and in 1928 a master's degree from Emory University. From 1899 to 1908, she was a professor and head of the science department at the Lucy Cobb Institute. This image of Woodberry is from the 1903 Lucy Cobb Institute yearbook. Her other accomplishments included being a founding member of both the Women's Press Club of Georgia and the Athens Women's Club. In 1908, she founded Woodberry Hall as a private school for girls. First located at the Grant Place on Peachtree and Pine Streets, the school moved to the newly constructed 50-room building on Peachtree Circle around 1914. By 1926, there were 12 faculty members, including Woodberry, who was the principal and taught English and the Bible. Woodberry Hall closed in 1932, shortly after its founder's death. (Courtesy of Hargrett Rare Books and Manuscript Library, University of Georgia Libraries.)

Woodberry Hall was built in 1914 by Mackle Construction Company, a prominent southeastern builder. The building permit, taken out by Rosa Woodberry, indicated an expected cost of $30,000. In the builder's photograph above, the recently constructed two-story brick building, with its 12 large white columns, is shown standing on a bleak hillside. To the right of the second flight of steps from the Peachtree Circle curb, one can see what appears to be a young girl, perhaps a Woodberry student. Below is a bird's-eye view of Woodberry Hall and its well-developed Peachtree Circle environs from around 1926. The school's playground and tennis court were probably located in the cleared area to the left and rear of the building. On the horizon, Stone Mountain is visible.

The Leyden House, located at 198 Peachtree Street, was constructed around 1858 for William Herring, a wealthy wholesale merchant. In September 1864, during the Union occupation of Atlanta, the house was used as the headquarters of Gen. George H. Thomas, commander of the Army of the Cumberland. In the above photograph, taken around 1864, Federal troops are seen leaning against two of the 12 Ionic columns. Made of cypress with iron bases, these fluted columns are reported to have contained hidden compartments used to cache valuables. When the Leyden House was torn down, the fluted columns were preserved through the efforts of Asa G. Chandler, the Coca-Cola magnate and philanthropist, and used in the construction of Woodberry Hall. The c. 1926 photograph at right shows the columns as seen from the 100-foot-long veranda.

Miss Woodberry's School for Girls was both a boarding school and a day school. The curriculum included English, Bible, music, athletics, foreign language, commercial, science, home economics, mathematics, and art. In 1926, the 22 graduating seniors were awarded a classical, general, or science diploma or a certificate in English. In her seventh-grade year, Margaret Mitchell attended Woodberry as a day student. This c. 1926 photograph shows part of the main hallway and the steps leading to the second-floor dormitory.

In the 1940s, the Woodberry Hall owners, Mr. and Mrs. Mooar, converted the building to apartments. In this postcard image, cars are parked on the front circular drive. An unidentified man and woman stand in a landscaped area below the drive. As today, the red bricks are painted white. (Courtesy of the Atlanta Time Machine.)

In 1935, Dorothy Alexander, grand dame of dance in Atlanta, moved to Woodberry Hall, where she lived for 48 years. In a 1983 interview with the *Atlanta Journal* she stated, "one of life's real gifts when I traveled a lot was to return to Ansley Park. I was touched by its beauty and its spirit." Alexander started her first school of ballet in Atlanta when she was only 18 years old. In 1929, she founded the Dorothy Alexander Concert Group, which, in the 1940s, became the Atlanta Civic Ballet, the first regional ballet company and the oldest continuously operating ballet company in the United States. When the company turned professional in 1967, the name was changed to the Atlanta Ballet. She is also credited with founding the nation's regional ballet movement. Faced with many hardships during her lifetime, Alexander was uplifted by reciting a poem by Grace Noll Crowell: "The day will bring some lovely thing/I say it over each new dawn/Some gay adventurous thing to hold/Against my heart until it's gone."

At the age of five, Dorothea Sydney Moses (Dorothy Alexander) was struck with osteomyelitis, an acute bone infection. After spending months in a hip cast, she relearned to walk. The recovery process led to dance, which she regarded as "a celebration of life." She studied in New York, London, and Atlanta and was a successful concert dancer prior to opening her first studio in Atlanta, La Petite École de Dance. The photograph at left from the 1930s shows Alexander performing as a ballerina, dancing en pointe. The below photograph, taken around 1945, is from the private scrapbook of Sybil Edwards McReynolds. A group of Alexander's students (identified as Bettye, Molly, Nancy, and Marianna) playfully pose for the camera outside what may have been Alexander's Woodberry Hall studio.

For over 50 years, Spring Street School was attended by the children of Ansley Park. Prior to its construction in 1919, the Tenth Street School (later Clark Howell School) was the elementary school closest to the suburb. Recognizing the need for a new school to serve the growing suburb, the city of Atlanta purchased land in the woods on unpaved Spring Street at Eighteenth Street. Nevertheless, a faction of Ansley Park residents wanted the school built within the suburb on its east side. Architect A. Ten Eyck Brown had designed a school for Ansley Park in 1909. This group offered to give the city land and finance the building of the school. Eugene Mitchell, the father of Margaret Mitchell, the Pulitzer Prize–winning author of *Gone With the Wind*, served on the board of education committee that made the final decision to build the school on the Spring Street land. In this June 1, 1936, photograph of Bobby (left) and David Gambrell, Spring Street School is visible in the background. (Courtesy of David Gambrell.)

Ivan Allen Jr., a future mayor of Atlanta (1962–1970), was a member of the third-grade class in the school's first year. Spring Street School closed in 1976. The facility is now home to the Center for Puppetry Arts, which was founded in 1978 by Vincent Anthony. According to this organization's website, "the Center has worked [since its inception] to serve the diverse populations

of Atlanta, the state of Georgia, and the country at large. The Center reaches the community through its focus on core programming: performance, Museum and education." This panoramic photograph is of the class of 1922. The yellow-bricked school is in the left background. (Courtesy of the Center for Puppetry Arts.)

This photograph, dated May 28, 1948, is of the Spring Street School faculty. Shown are, from left to right, (first row) two unidentified, Mrs. Clifton, unidentified, and Miss Costello; (second row) Mrs. Dillard, Miss Cannon, Mrs. Douglas (principal), Miss Penick, and unidentified; (third row) Mrs. Young, unidentified, Mrs. Bigham (cafeteria), two unidentified, and Mrs. Cook. (Courtesy of the Center for Puppetry Arts.)

Miss Costello's 1948 third-grade class poses for a photograph. Shown are, from left to right, (first row) Craig, Gaines, Chambers, Bosard, Craig, Atkinson, and Yates; (second row) Lewis, Young, Chastain, Rosselot, Berman, Anderson, Bates, and Bryant; (third row) Gunsard, Hagerman, Norwood, Ginsback, Lanier, Glass, Robinson, and Dewitt; (fourth row) Miss Costello, Sallwe (?), Wilcox, Girvan, Bullard, Neely, Goodrich, and Lanier. (Courtesy of the Center for Puppetry Arts.)

The above photograph, dated May 7, 1951, shows Mrs. Dillard's fourth-grade class at Spring Street School. Shown are, from left to right, (first row) Wright, Norwood, Blackman, Peace, Arnold, and Bridges; (second row) Lane, Manning, Cameron, Peters, Johnson, McClatchey, Gates, and Brown; (third row) Suratt, Avent, Pelot, Kelly, Little, Mundorf, Mrs. Dillard, Landers, Smith, Wilde, and unidentified. The below photograph, taken around 1950, includes Fay Pearce's sixth-grade teacher, Julia Clifton (right), her daughter (left), and an elderly woman who Tallulah Reed Lyons remembers as someone the class would visit and entertain with their singing. The children are Julia Clifton's granddaughters. (Above, courtesy of the Center for Puppetry Arts; below, courtesy of E. Fay Pearce Jr.)

Miss Shaw's morning kindergarten class at Spring Street School (above) poses for a photograph on May 23, 1944. Among the identified are, from left to right, (first row) Warren (center); (second row) Pearce (far right); (third row) Moore, Hall, Maier, Johnson, unidentified, Woodall, Cole, unidentified, and Roberts; (fourth row) Miss Shaw (far left), Roberts (fourth from left), and Reed (far right). The author attended Spring Street School from kindergarten through seventh grade. In the below photograph of Mrs. Wallace's kindergarten class, dated March 12, 1954, he is in the third row, third from right. (Above, courtesy of Tallulah Reed Lyons; below, author's collection.)

Nine

GOVERNORS

In 1910, Edwin P. Ansley built his 14-room, five-bath, 10,000-square-foot mansion in the subdivision he was developing. Described as an Early English residence, the granite-rock, green-tile-roof, fortress-like structure was designed by the architect A. Ten Eyck Brown. Sitting on a hill 40 feet above street level, Ansley's mansion at 205 The Prado was an imposing residence. Edwin and his family lived there until his death in 1923. In 1925, the house became the Georgia governor's mansion, first under a lease and shortly thereafter purchased for $86,000. Clifford Walker was the first governor to live on The Prado. Subsequent executive residents included governors Lamartine Hardman, Richard B. Russell, Eugene Talmadge, E.D. Rivers, Ellis Arnall, Melvin Thompson, Herman Talmadge, Marvin Griffin, Ernest Vandiver Jr., Carl Sanders, and Lester Maddox. In 1967, Governor Maddox, the last Georgia governor to live on The Prado, moved to the new governor's mansion in Buckhead. The main building was demolished in 1969. Only the renovated two-story carriage house remains.

Clifford Mitchell Walker (left), who served as governor of Georgia from 1923 to 1927, won election primarily due to his support for the reemerged Ku Klux Klan, which he promised to protect and subsequently joined. The Georgia Forestry Commission was created during his administration. Following his tenure as governor, he lived on Fifteenth Street. Lamartine Griffin Hardman (below), governor from 1927 to 1931, was a successful physician, businessman, and farmer. Partially due to his inability to finesse the general assembly, he had few legislative accomplishments. The simplification of state government, which he initiated, was implemented by his successor. (Left, courtesy of the Georgia Archives, Georgia Capital Museum Collection, 1992.23.0058; below, courtesy of the Georgia Archives, Small Print Collection, spc17-044.)

Richard Brevard Russell Jr. was one of Georgia's most influential leaders. After earning a law degree in 1918 from the University of Georgia, he practiced law in his hometown of Winder, Georgia. Prior to being elected governor, he served for 10 years in the Georgia House of Representatives, four years as speaker. Elected governor in 1930, he served from 1931 to 1933. Under his leadership, the Reorganization Act of 1931 was passed. This legislation resulted in a number of cost-cutting reforms that included the elimination of 85 state agencies and the creation of a board of regents for state-supported colleges. After leaving the governorship, Russell served for 38 distinguished years in the US Senate, where he became highly influential in national affairs and third in line for the US presidency. A master at political compromise, he served on the Armed Services Committee, where for 16 years he was the chairman, and on the powerful Appropriations Committee. He opposed the Civil Rights Act and initially opposed sending troops to Vietnam. (Courtesy of the Georgia Archives, Vanishing Georgia Collection, brw279-86.)

Holding office from 1933 to 1937 and from 1941 to 1943, Eugene Talmadge was only the second Georgia governor elected four times. Given to flamboyant behavior and passionate speeches, his critics called him "the Wild Man from Sugar Creek." A forceful and dogmatic leader, Talmadge put down a textile strike by declaring martial law, fired the public service commission over high utility rates, and purged the board of regents for refusing to dismiss educators who supported integration. He opposed civil rights, labor unions, and federal government controls. At left, Henry Ford, the assembly-line innovator and automobile executive, appears to be signing a guest register while Talmadge and Ford's wife, Clara Bryant, stand watching. Below, Talmadge and Ford are walking together. Both photographs were taken in the Ansley Park governor's mansion around 1935.

Eurith Dickinson Rivers served Georgia as governor for two terms (1937–1941). According to James F. Cook, writing in *The Governors of Georgia, 1754–1995*, having taken office "in the midst of the Great Depression, [Rivers] supported President Franklin Roosevelt with unrestrained enthusiasm and is credited with bringing the New Deal to Georgia." The accomplishments of his administration include participation in the national rural electrification program, and creation of the State Housing Authority, Rural Housing Authority, and the State Hospital Authority. Denied tax increases needed to support his many programs, Rivers instituted a number of budget cuts but nevertheless left office with a large deficit. At right, Rivers is wearing his trademark black bowtie. Below, he is addressing a group in Union County, Georgia, around 1939. (Right, courtesy of the Georgia Archives, Small Print Collection, spc31-001; below, courtesy of the Georgia Archives, Vanishing Georgia Collection, uni005.)

When elected in 1943, Ellis Gibbs Arnall was, at 35, the youngest governor in the nation. During his administration (1943–1947), a new state constitution was adopted, the state university system's accreditation was restored, and the state penal system was modernized. Here, Arnall (bottom right) is meeting with three members of the LaGrange Junior Chamber of Commerce (standing) and Cason Callaway. (Courtesy of the Georgia Archives, Vanishing Georgia Collection, trp208.)

In 1946, Eugene Talmadge was again elected governor; Melvin Ernest Thompson was elected lieutenant governor. When Talmadge died before his inauguration, Thompson assumed the governorship. However, the Georgia General Assembly elected Talmadge's son, Herman. This debacle, called the "three governors dispute," was subsequently resolved in Thompson's favor by the Georgia Supreme Court. Here, Thompson (center, holding hat) and Herman Talmadge (right) are seen during the dispute in 1947. (Courtesy of the Georgia Archives, Vanishing Georgia Collection, geo036.)

The portrait at right of Gov. Melvin Thompson (1947–1948) hangs in the capitol building. Herman Eugene Talmadge, who served as governor of Georgia from 1948 to 1955, is shown below around 1950 giving a spirited speech in Lawrenceville, Georgia. Talmadge easily defeated Thompson in a special election held on September 8, 1948. In 1956, Talmadge was elected to the US Senate, an office he held for 24 years. During his long tenure in national office, he played a key role in the passage of important legislation and held the influential position of chairman of the Agriculture Committee. According to James A. Cook, his wise questioning and analyses during the 1973 Watergate investigation elevated his reputation; he was "one of the more powerful and respected statesmen in the nation." (Right, courtesy of the Georgia Archives, Capitol Museum Collection, 1992.23.0065; below, courtesy of the Georgia Archives, Vanishing Georgia Collection, gwn285.)

Samuel Marvin Griffin served as governor of Georgia from 1955 to 1959. As was the case with many of his predecessors, he was a staunch segregationist. With the increased revenues provided by a state sales tax, Griffin greatly expanded government services. His administration was scandalized by corruption. Here, Griffin (center) poses with a group of McDuffie County politicians in the 1950s. (Courtesy of the Georgia Archives, Vanishing Georgia Collection, mcd018.)

Standing before a crowd of supporters in 1958 are Texas Senator and future US President Lyndon B. Johnson (left), Georgia Governor-elect Ernest Vandiver (center), and Georgia Senator Herman Talmadge.

Samuel Ernest Vandiver served as governor from 1959 to 1963. His initial focus was on restoring public confidence. However, his biggest challenge occurred in 1961, when a federal judge ordered the University of Georgia to admit two black students. Following Georgia law, Vandiver closed the university. After meeting with his top advisors at the mansion, Vandiver showed great leadership when he reversed his position and reopened the school. (Courtesy of the Georgia Archives, RG4-10-74, bq0022.)

Carl Edward Sanders, the first Georgia governor elected by popular vote, focused on improving the quality of education. According to James F. Cook, Sanders provided "a voice of reason, moderation, and common sense [during] . . . this turbulent and chaotic period [and] . . . emerged as a leader of the New South." In this undated photograph, Governor Sanders (second from right) is making an official presentation. He served from 1963 to 1967. (Courtesy of the Georgia Archives, Small Print Collection, spc18-064a.)

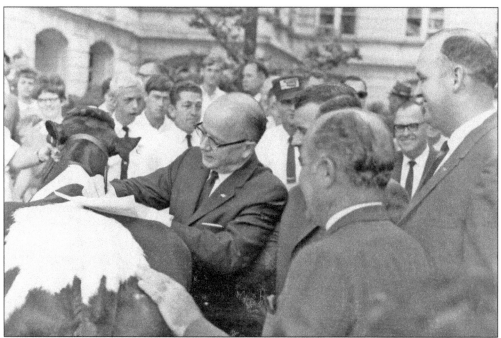

Lester Garfield Maddox was the last governor to reside in Ansley Park. With only a tenth-grade education, he built his Pickrick Restaurant into one of the largest eating establishments in Atlanta. A fanatical segregationist, he closed the restaurant rather than serve African Americans. In the general election, neither he nor his opponent gained the required majority. The often bizarre-acting Maddox was then elected governor by the general assembly. He served from 1967 to 1971. The above photograph, taken around 1970 in front of the Georgia state capital, shows Maddox signing a document on the back of a cow. Below, the governor's mansion is decorated for the Christmas holiday around 1945. The author fondly remembers his family's annual Christmas light tour, which included riding through the nearby Sherwood Forest neighborhood and then past the mansion. (Above, courtesy of the Georgia Archives, Georgia Capitol Collection, 2003.0278a.6.)

BIBLIOGRAPHY

Ansley Park: 100 Years of Gracious Living. The Ansley Park Civic Association, 2004.

Ansley Park Homes. Atlanta: Byrd Printing Company, undated.

Bassett, Beth Dawkins and Gayle White. *A Church on Peachtree: First Presbyterian Church of Atlanta, A Sesquicentennial Story 1884–1998.* First Presbyterian Church of Atlanta, 1998, 2011.

Beard, Rick. *From Suburb to Defended Neighborhood: Change in Atlanta's Inman Park and Ansley Park, 1890–1980.* Doctoral Dissertation, Emory University, 1981.

Blumberg, Janice Rothschild. *As But a Day to A Hundred and Twenty, 1867–1987.* Atlanta: Hebrew Benevolent Congregation, 1966, 1987.

Cook, James F. *The Governors of Georgia, 1754–1995.* Macon, GA: Mercer University Press, 1995.

Davis, Paul K. *100 Decisive Battles: From Ancient Times to the Present.* New York and Oxford, UK: Oxford University Press, 1999.

Ecelbarger, Gary. *The Day Dixie Died.* New York: Thomas Dunne Books, 2010.

Edwards, Anne. *Road to Tara: The Life of Margaret Mitchell.* Boston: G.K. Hall & Co., 1983.

Encyclopedia Britannica. Available at: www.britannica.com.

Farr, Finis. *Margaret Mitchell of Atlanta.* New York: Avon Books, 1974.

Garrett, Franklin M. *Atlanta and Environs: A Chronicle of People and Events.* 3 vols. Atlanta: Lewis Historical Publishing Company, 1954; reprint ed. Athens: University of Georgia Press, 1969.

Garrett, Franklin M. *Yesterday's Atlanta.* Miami: E.A. Seemann Publishing, 1974.

Mitchell, William R. Jr. *J. Neel Reid Architect of Hentz, Reid & Adler and the Georgia School of Classicists.* The Georgia Trust For Historic Preservation, 1997.

New Georgia Encyclopedia. Available at www.georgiaencyclopedia.org.

Pyron, Darden Asbury. *Southern Daughter: The Life of Margaret Mitchell.* New York and Oxford, UK: Oxford University Press, 1991.

Schmidt, Diane Hopper, ed. *A Century of Better Care: 100 Years of Piedmont Hospital.* Atlanta: Piedmont Hospital, 2004.

Swann, David. *Ansley Golf Club: "One Hell of a Good Club."* The Ansley Golf Club, 1999.

Visit us at
arcadiapublishing.com

Printed in the USA
CPSIA information can be obtained
at www.ICGtesting.com
LVHW081333140823
755100LV00079B/114

9 781531 667825